The Roman Empire
under
Emperor Trajan

Ephesus

Antioch

Jerusalem

Alexandria

The borders of the
Roman Empire
in the
Low Countries

KATWIJK
VOORBURG
LEIDEN
WOERDEN
ALPHEN
A/D RIJN
UTRECHT

NIJMEGEN

MAASTRICHT

COLOGNE

First published in Belgium and Holland by Clavis Uitgeverij,
Hasselt – Amsterdam, 2014
Copyright © 2014, Clavis Uitgeverij

English translation from the Dutch by Clavis Publishing Inc. New York
Copyright © 2017 for the English language edition: Clavis Publishing Inc. New York

Visit us on the web at www.clavisbooks.com

Want to Know. The Romans written by Suzan Boshouwers, objects illustrated by Suzan Boshouwers,
illustrated by Veronica Nahmias
Original title: *Willewete. Romeinen*
Translated from the Dutch by Clavis Publishing

ISBN 978-1-60537-319-5

This book was printed in October 2016 at Graspo CZ, a.s.,
Pod Šternberkem 324, 76302 Zlín, Czech Republic

First Edition
10 9 8 7 6 5 4 3 2 1

Clavis Publishing supports the First Amendment
and celebrates the right to read

Want to know
history

The Romans

Suzan Boshouwers & Veronica Nahmias

Clavis

NEW YORK

golden helmet

Look! Theo and his little sister are digging a deep hole. Theo hopes he'll find something from Roman times. The Romans are an ancient people. They lived all over Europe a very long time ago. You can still find traces of them under the ground.

Did you know
three shoes were found
near the golden helmet?
This is one of them. They
probably belonged to
soldiers too.

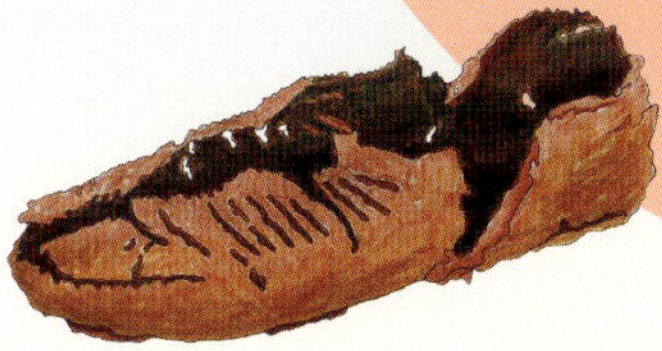

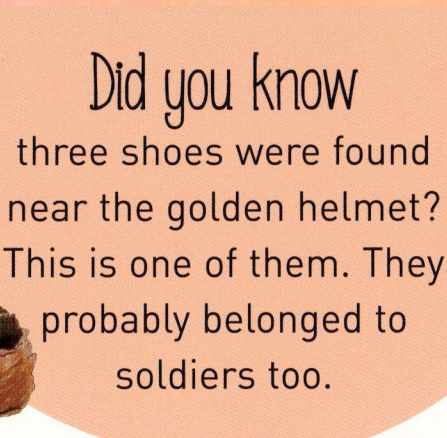

This is where we're from

The Romans rule over a great empire: a large part of Europe and even a part of Africa. Everywhere Roman soldiers go, they raid villages. The people that live there have to obey them. Right in the middle of the Roman Empire lies Rome, the biggest and wealthiest city in the entire world, with busy streets and temples and a big race track called a circus. Rome is the home of many important people who rule the empire. The emperor is in charge. To the right, you see Emperor Trajan. Statues of him can be found in nearly every city.

getting water

fighting practice

carts

inspecting weapons

Did you know
the Romans lived about
two thousand years ago?

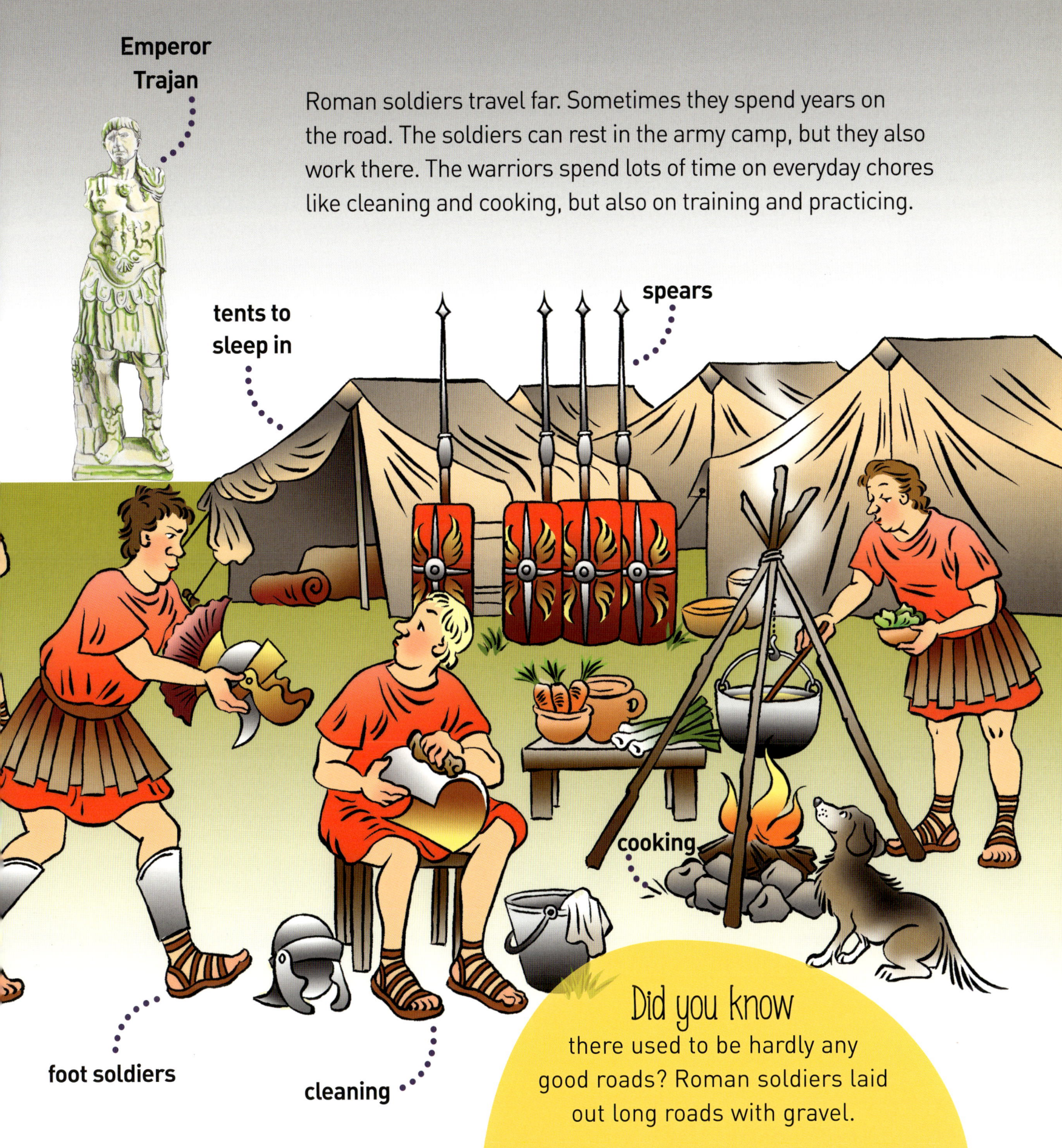

Emperor Trajan

Roman soldiers travel far. Sometimes they spend years on the road. The soldiers can rest in the army camp, but they also work there. The warriors spend lots of time on everyday chores like cleaning and cooking, but also on training and practicing.

spears

tents to sleep in

cooking

foot soldiers

cleaning

Did you know there used to be hardly any good roads? Roman soldiers laid out long roads with gravel.

This is what a Roman soldier looks like

mask

bugler

cuirass

animal skin

sandals

shield

belt
(this jingles when you walk, so people know you're coming)

A Roman soldier tries his best to look as impressive as possible. The enemy has to believe he can never beat these strong soldiers. It's because of Roman soldiers that this empire is so big. The soldiers are very good at working together. These warriors hold shields in front of, next to and on top of themselves: that way they're protected nearly everywhere. How could you ever beat them? This is called "fighting in testudo formation" or "fighting in tortoise formation". Can you guess why?

lance

helmet

amulet

sword

Did you know a legion consists of six thousand soldiers?

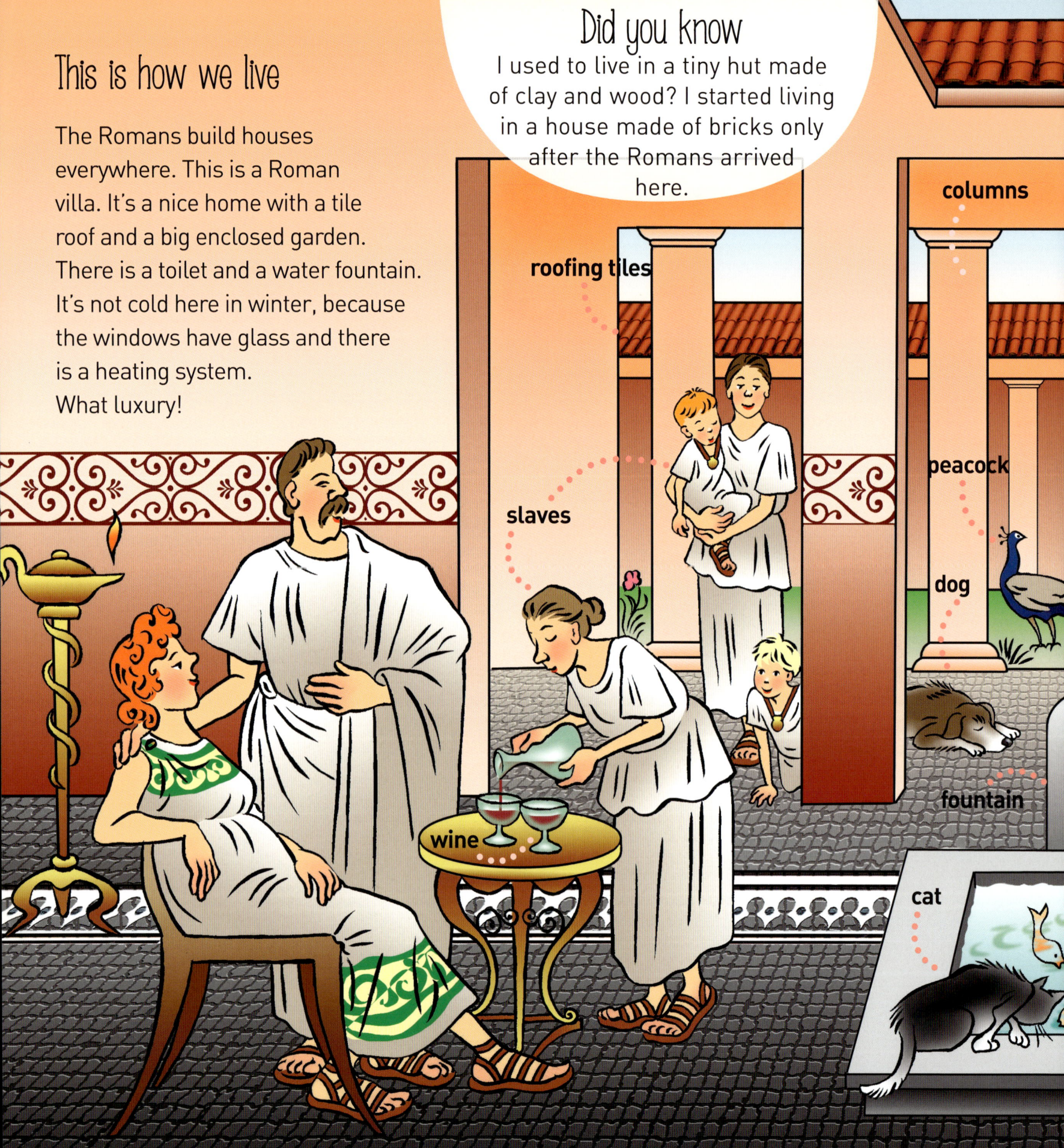

This is how we live

The Romans build houses everywhere. This is a Roman villa. It's a nice home with a tile roof and a big enclosed garden. There is a toilet and a water fountain. It's not cold here in winter, because the windows have glass and there is a heating system.
What luxury!

Did you know

I used to live in a tiny hut made of clay and wood? I started living in a house made of bricks only after the Romans arrived here.

columns

roofing tiles

peacock

slaves

dog

wine

fountain

cat

pot with
a face

A big family lives in this villa. The slaves that belong to the family live in this house too. Everyone has his own bedroom. The villa has a dining room with a mosaic floor, wall paintings and beautiful serving vessels. One of the pots has a face.

curtain

crow

wall paintings

oil lamp

serving vessels

day bed
with pillow

pond with
fish

To the market

We go to the market often. It's very busy. There are many stalls with delicious things to choose from: bread, olive oil, herbs like thyme and oregano, and fruit. At the market, we usually pay with coins made of copper or silver. Some are even made of gold.

butcher

meat

donkey

baker

geese

shaving

chicken

cat

Look, this coin has the head of Emperor Trajan on it. You can also get wine at the market. Every Roman drinks wine, even the children. Wine is made from grapes that grow here. Some things sold at the market come from other places, such as the colored fabrics: they are brought here on a ship.

golden coin

trading

wine seller

fish

fabrics

paying

fruit

scales
(to weigh the coins)

Did you know
the Romans travel all across the world for trade? When they return from their long trips, they often bring back beautiful things, like jewels and gemstones.

Did you know
Romans don't always pay with coins? Sometimes they trade things for other things.

This is my day

1 The day starts with washing. We are rich, so we have running water.

2 Next, the slaves help me get dressed.

3 The slaves help my father shave.

perfume bottle

4 And the slaves help my mother with her hair, make-up and perfume.

5 Our house has an altar. It contains a statue of our household goddess. We place wine, cookies, flowers and food in front of her. We hope she will protect us. The altar is a sacred place. Look! There's a light in it!

6   Poor children in the Roman Empire can't read or write. I get to go to school. We learn how to read and write in Latin and in Greek. And we learn mathematics.

7   The evening meal is a nice part of the day. The whole family is together. We eat while reclining, like all Romans do. First our feet are washed.

Did you know
the Romans wrote numbers differently from us? An I means one, a V means five and a X means ten!

rattle

8   One of our slaves gives my little sister her food.

Did you know
Roman children wear amulets around their necks? We believe that amulets keep us healthy and protect us from danger.

There is so much to see on the street. Look for yourself!

1. mosaic
2. well
3. toilet
4. building
5. stones
6. slaves
7. marble
8. columns
9. Roman numerals
10. statue
11. temple
12. goldsmith
13. getting water
14. butcher
15. paving bricks
16. games
17. scribe
18. merchant
19. litter
20. cart
21. roofing tiles
22. fountain
23. talking
24. furniture maker
25. potter
26. goat cart
27. water carrier
28. donkey
29. dogs
30. cat

The story of Romulus and Remus

Every Roman child knows the story
of Romulus and Remus....

A long time ago,
a she-wolf lived
near the Tiber.
That's a big river in Italy.
One day she heard
a strange sound.
She went to see where
it came from.

Then she saw
a basket floating
in the water.
There were two babies
in the basket. They were
Romulus and Remus.
They were crying with
cold and hunger.

The she-wolf
pulled the basket out
of the water, took
the babies to
her warm den
and let them drink.
The wolf took care of
them like a real
mother.

Later a
shepherd came by.
He saw the boys near the
den and took them
to his hut to take further
care of them. Years went by.
When Romulus and Remus
became men,
they went back to the Tiber.
In that very same spot,
they wanted to build a city.

But the city did not yet have a name. Then the brothers had a disagreement. Remus wanted the city to have his name, but Romulus wanted the city to be named after *him*. They started fighting, and Remus was killed. Romulus became the first king of the city! The city was called Rome and is still called Rome to this very day.

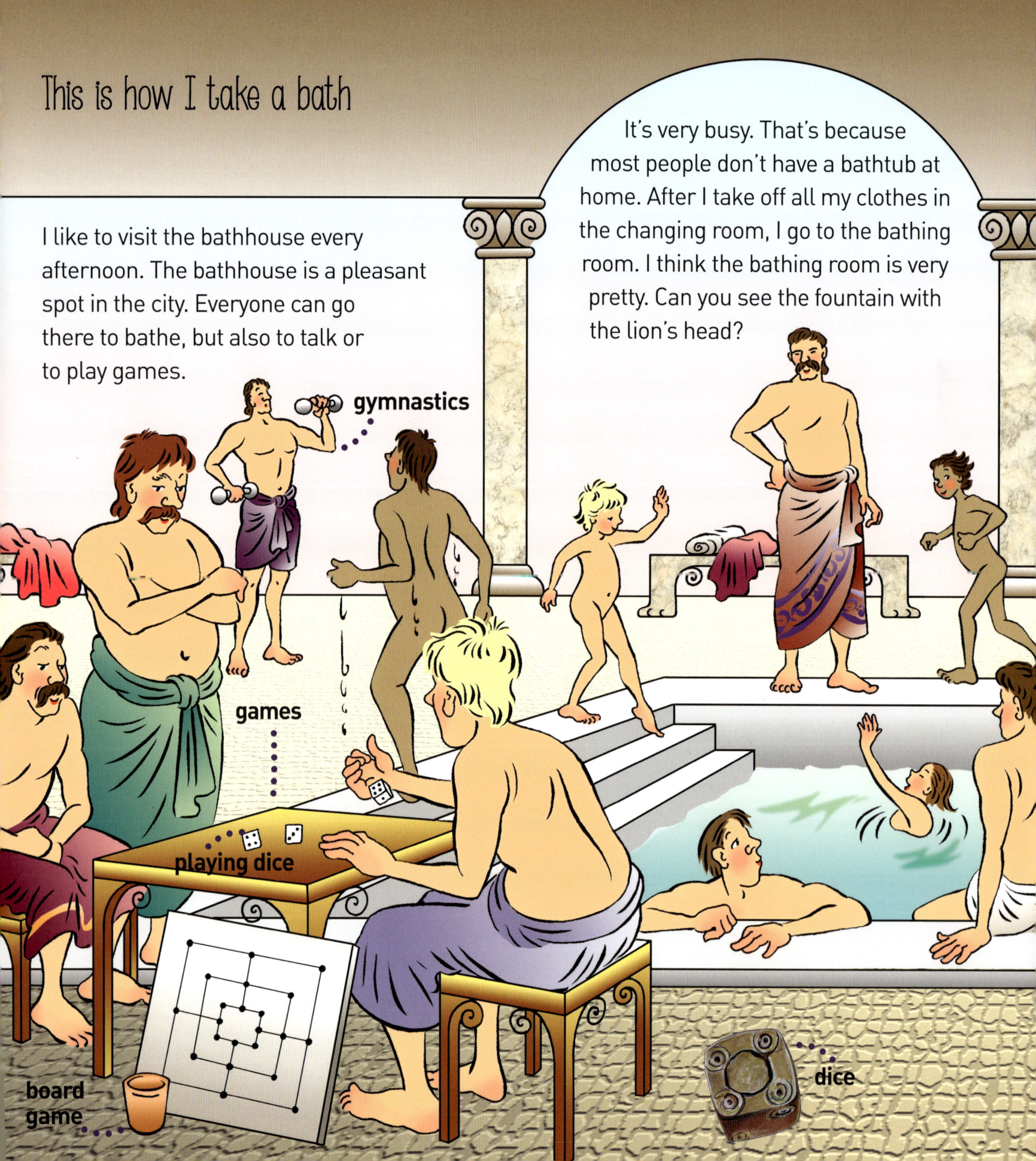

This is how I take a bath

I like to visit the bathhouse every afternoon. The bathhouse is a pleasant spot in the city. Everyone can go there to bathe, but also to talk or to play games.

It's very busy. That's because most people don't have a bathtub at home. After I take off all my clothes in the changing room, I go to the bathing room. I think the bathing room is very pretty. Can you see the fountain with the lion's head?

gymnastics

games

playing dice

board game

dice

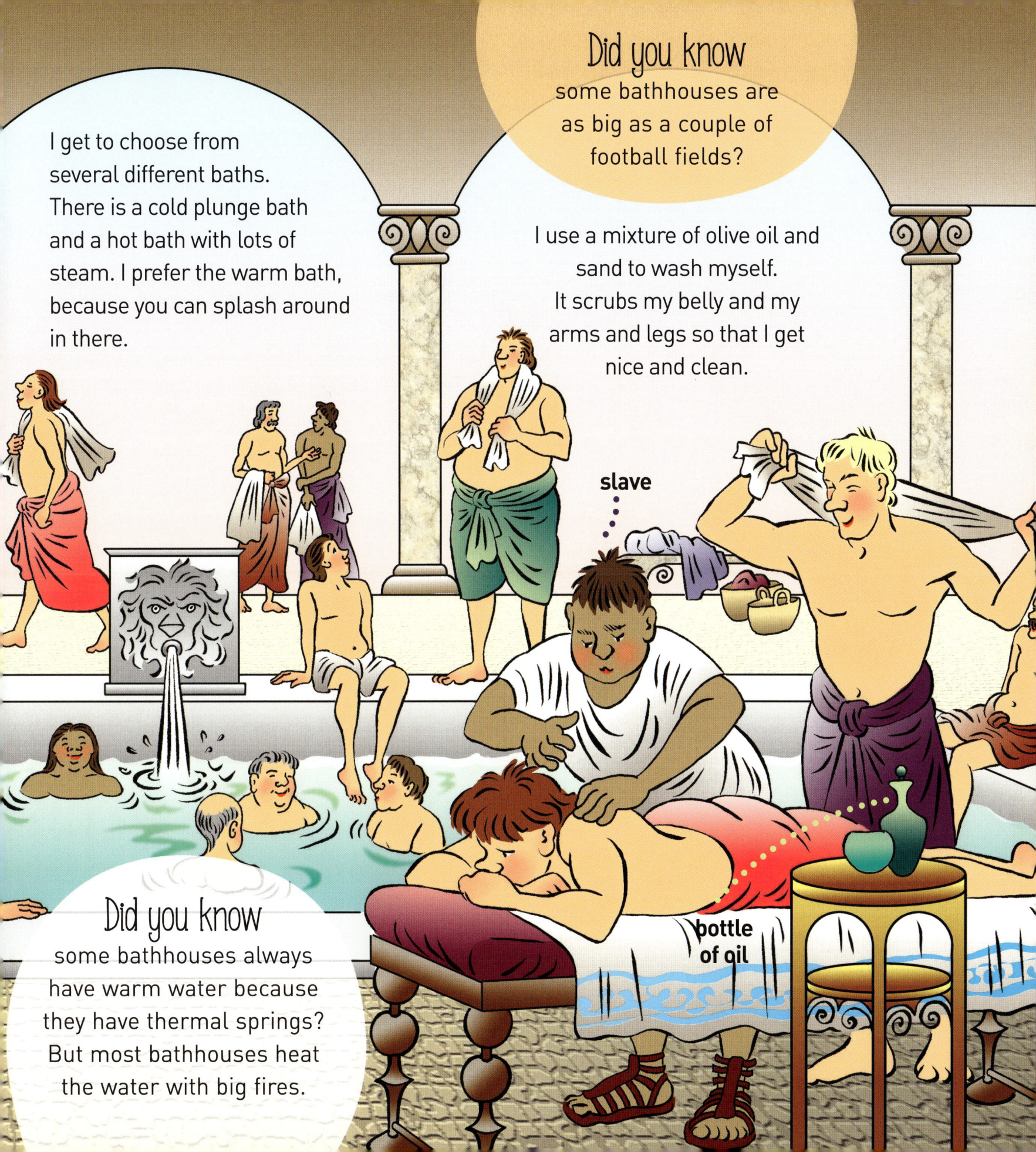

priest

This is what our temples look like

The temples are the Romans' nicest buildings. Romans have many gods and they all need a house. That's why the Romans build a lot of temples for them. And of course, they have to be as beautiful as possible.

The gods play an important role in the lives of the Romans. They bring us health, luck, wisdom and other things we value. Nearly every day we visit a temple to offer gifts to the gods. We believe that this will make them look after us.

oil lamp

Did you know
we believe that an emperor
becomes a god after he dies?
He gets his own temple then.

This is how we celebrate

Today is a feast day to honor the goddess Ceres. We hold a procession for her today.
That's a long parade. Everybody is dressed nicely and there is music.
The procession moves all through the city.

trumpet

decoration

incense

fruit (as an offering)

sacrificial animals

The goddess Ceres is very important to us. For instance, she makes sure that there's always enough to eat. The animals walking along in the parade are sacrificial animals. We offer them to the goddess to thank her so that she will continue to help us.

fan (to keep flies and bugs away)

drum

flute

priest

Did you know the Romans also introduced chickens to Northern Europe?

So many gods!

Apollo: God of art, sunlight and music.

Venus: Goddess of love and beauty.

Vulcan: God of fire, metalworkers and volcanoes.

Pluto: God of the underworld.

Neptune: God of the sea.

Jupiter: King of all gods. God of the sky and thunder. Juno's husband.

Minerva: Goddess of wisdom and thought.

Ceres: Goddess of fertility.

Mini-quiz

1. What does 'Ave' mean?

2. What is the tortoise formation?

3. Why aren't Roman villas cold in winter?

4. What's the most important city in the Roman Empire?

5. Do Romans only pay with coins at the market?

6. Why do Roman children wear amulets?

7. Who raised Romulus and Remus when they were babies?

8. Why do Romans visit the bathhouse?

9. What planets are named after Roman gods?

10. Which Roman god is the king of the gods?

So many nice things!

In this book you saw drawings of objects from the times of the ancient Romans. Here you can read more about these things and about where they were found.
Most of the items were found in or near the Netherlands, the home country of author Suzan Boshouwers.

Rattle

This is a rattle. It contains small pebbles. If you move it from side to side, it makes a funny noise. What animal does the rattle look like? Is it a bird, or an animal with long ears?

Found in: Nijmegen (the Netherlands)

Golden coin

This coin was found in the Netherlands. It has the head of Emperor Trajan on it. The coin is made out of gold.

Found in: Woerden (Utrecht, the Netherlands)

Pot with face

The Romans used this pot as a drinking cup. The face was probably meant to keep away evil spirits.

Found in: Woerden (Utrecht, the Netherlands)

Shoe

Three shoes were found near the helmet. Two for a right foot and one for a left foot. Isn't that strange? The shoes are made of leather and were probably worn by Roman soldiers, just like the helmet.

Found in: de Peel (North Brabant, the Netherlands)

Oil lamp

The handle of this pretty oil lamp is decorated with a horse's head. Oil lamps were often placed on altars for the gods.

Found in: Doorwerth (Gelderland, the Netherlands)